Sports Illustrated
SQUASH

The Sports Illustrated Library

Sports Illustrated
SQUASH

BY THE EDITORS OF
SPORTS ILLUSTRATED

J. B. LIPPINCOTT COMPANY

Philadelphia and New York

1971

ISBN–0–397–00837–6 Cloth Ed
ISBN–0–397–00838–4 Paper Ed

Fourth Printing

Photographs from *Sports Illustrated*, © Time, Inc.

Photographs on pages 8, 14, 18, 32, 46 and 72 by James Drake.

Photographs on front cover and page 24 by Richard Lerner.

Contents

Text by Al Malloy, Jr., with Rex Lardner
Illustrations by Frank Mullins

Sports Illustrated
SQUASH

1
The Game

THE ORIGINS of racquets—the ancestor game of squash racquets—are veiled in antiquity, but it is known that the game was a pastime of debtors in Fleet Prison in 19th-century London. Now commonly known as just "squash" (a term derived from the squashy sound of the ball formerly used on hitting a wall), the game was introduced to America in the 1890s and rapidly spread to become one of this country's most popular indoor sports. It affords a quick, pleasant workout, and the beginner can have as good a time as the expert.

The main rules are simple. To be good, a shot must strike the front wall between the telltale and the topmost red line before hitting the floor. It may hit the side walls or back wall before reaching the front wall. The ball must be struck before it has bounced twice, but it may be struck on the volley. A ball reaching the back wall on the fly may be hit after it has bounced on the floor.

Either the server or receiver may score. The winner of a point serves the following point. With two exceptions,

9

the first player to get 15 points wins a game. However, if the score reaches 13-all, the player who lost the tying point "sets" the game at either 15, 16 or 18 points; the winner is the player who first reaches the selected number. (If "no set" is declared, the game is 15 points.) If the score reaches 14-all without first having reached 13-all, the loser of the tying point may set the game at 15 or 17.

A game is begun by spinning a racket to see who serves first. The server may begin serving on either side of the court—standing with one foot inside the serving quarter circle—thereafter alternating sides. From the backhand, or left, side of the court he serves to the forehand, or right, side and vice versa. To be good, a serve must hit the front wall between the front wall service line and the topmost red line before hitting any other surface and must land within the lines of the proper service court. A second serve is permitted if the first is a fault. A double fault costs the server one point and the service. Service lines and quarter

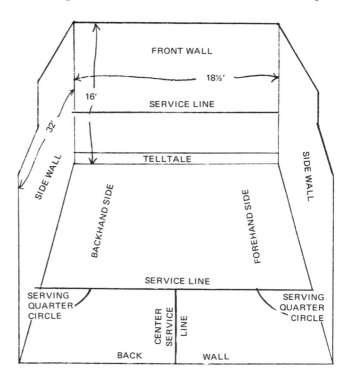

circles have no significance once the receiver has hit the ball. The serve may be taken on the volley.

A let is called when one player interferes with his opponent's stroke or passage to the ball, and the point is replayed. A let is also called when one player refrains from swinging his racket lest he strike his opponent.

When a player is struck by a ball coming off his opponent's racket, various rulings apply. If the ball had been headed for the front wall, the striker wins the point. If the ball would have hit a side wall before hitting the front wall, the point is replayed. If the ball would not have hit the front wall, the striker loses the point. The striker loses the point if he is hit by his own ball.

Tactically, the floor is divided into four parts: Forecourt, midcourt, backcourt and center. Most points are won by offensive shots made in the forecourt and midcourt. The center—called the T—is the best point from which to await a return. Shots that force one's opponent, in making his

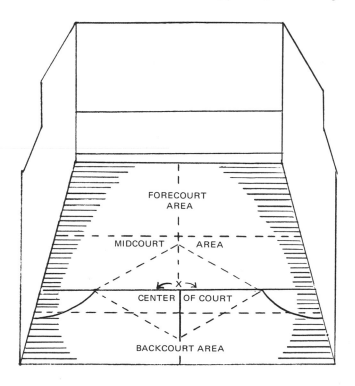

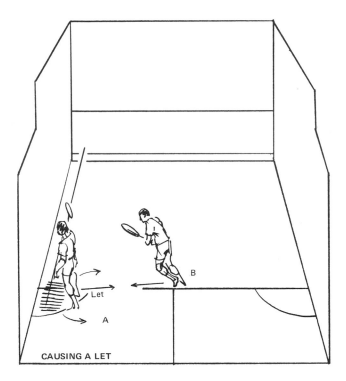

CAUSING A LET

return, to cut through the diamond-shaped area in the diagram on page 11 should be avoided, as the player who has hit the ball must then abandon the center.

Courtesy to one's adversary is a vital element of squash. Each player must give his opponent free access to the ball and room to swing—even at the cost of placing himself at a tactical disadvantage. Moreover, it is imperative that each player know the position of his opponent before making his stroke. Failure to heed this unwritten rule can result in a serious accident. Every player should consider courtesy his major obligation.

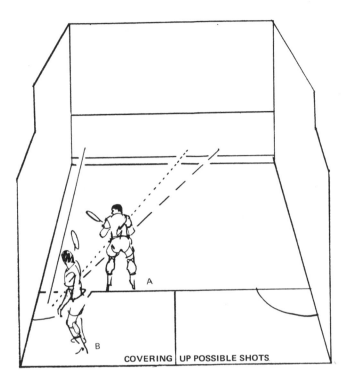

COVERING | UP POSSIBLE SHOTS

Two common discourtesies are shown on these pages. In the drawing on the left, A, after hitting a hard rail shot, should not head directly for the T but should avoid a collision by circling behind or in front of B. In the drawing at the right, A is "covering up" several possible shots by B, gaining an unfair tactical advantage. Since discourtesy may breed not only further discourtesy but possible injury, the squash player must be a sportsman.

2
The Grip

SINCE squash is essentially a game of fast wrist action and delicate touch, great care must be taken to hold the racket correctly—even if the grip at first feels unnatural. Failure to hold the racket correctly, no matter how skillful a player is, will limit his ability to hit the immense variety of offensive and defensive shots used in squash.

The grip used by most top-ranking players—the one which I recommend—is the versatile Continental grip (p. 16), which allows shots to be taken on both the forehand and backhand, off the floor and on the volley, without changing the position of the fingers. This is an important feature, since rallies in squash are often so fast that there is no time to change from one grip to another.

Other advantages of the Continental grip are that it permits easy movement of the wrist in a horizontal plane, is ideal for hitting the ball at a height between the ankles and the knees—where most shots are taken—and permits the arm, wrist and hand to be extended to their fullest without strain or awkwardness. Finally, it makes it easy

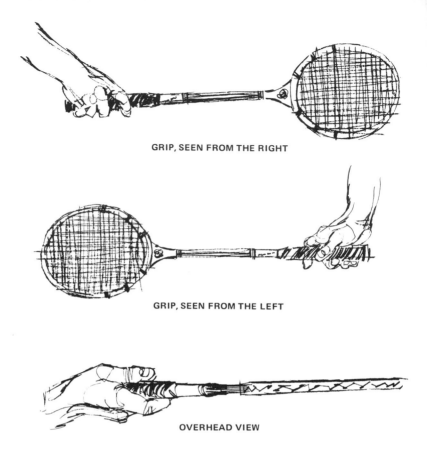

GRIP, SEEN FROM THE RIGHT

GRIP, SEEN FROM THE LEFT

OVERHEAD VIEW

to give the ball the slight underspin that is characteristic of most shots in squash.

TO GET A PROPER CONTINENTAL GRIP

1. Hold the racket throat in the left hand, with the racket face perpendicular to the floor. 2. Place the right hand on the handle as though about to pick up a hammer. The heel of the hand should be placed slightly to the right of the center of the handle. 3. Spread the fingers slightly, particularly the index finger and the thumb. These fingers

16

supply most of the control of the racket head. If, at this point, there is a "palming" feel to the grip, correct it by allowing the racket to slip down in the fingers.

In the final position, the racket should lie diagonally across the palm of the hand, with pressure felt mainly at three points: On the inner part of the thumb, the inner part of the forefinger and the heel of the hand. Slight pressure should be felt on the second joint of the third finger and less on the remaining fingers.

In stroking, the racket should be held firmly, not tightly. An overly tight grip locks the wrist and builds tension.

SELECTING A RACKET

In squash, as opposed to tennis, selection of a racket is determined more by the feel of the grip than the size of the grip or the racket's weight. The beginner should select a racket a shade on the heavy side—one weighing about 9½ ounces when strung. Its grip should be a little larger than that favored by the experienced player. The reason for this is that persons playing the game the first few times have a tendency, because of the relatively light weight of the racket, to use the wrist a great deal, though not always correctly.

A slightly larger grip will help control the movement of the wrist and prevent the formation of bad habits. As the player increases in skill and learns wrist control, along with the proper timing of his shots, he may wish to purchase a racket with a smaller grip.

The type of game favored by the player—retrieving, hard-hitting or volleying—will also determine the kind of racket later selected. A hard-hitter prefers a racket heavy in the head; a player who volleys frequently likes a light racket which is light in the head.

The racket should be strung with gut. Although a press is not necessary, it is a good idea to place a cover on the racket when it is not in use to preserve the strings.

3
The Ready Position

IN SQUASH the ball often comes off the front and side walls so fast that a player must be completely alert and ready to move into position to hit it. If he is slow, the ball will be past him or will have bounced twice, or its speed will force him to make a weak return. One of the most favored tactics, indeed, is to return the ball so quickly to an opponent that he is caught unaware and cannot make a proper, well-placed shot.

It is necessary then, before your opponent hits the ball, to assume a position of readiness, all senses alert, so that no time is lost in getting to the ball and returning it.

This is the position recommended before actually moving to the ball and stroking it:

Stand in the center of the court (each heel about one inch in front of the floor service line), facing the front wall. Heels should be no farther apart than the width of the shoulders. Weight should be evenly distributed and resting on the balls of the feet—not on the toes, as this

produces tension in the calves and thighs. The feet should be turned slightly outward, allowing you to step toward the ball with the nearest foot without loss of time.

It is extremely important to crouch. The knees are bent, the spine is straight and the body leans slightly forward. The head is raised. The position is one of keen anticipation, like that of a tennis player expecting to receive a hard service or a shortstop ready to spring toward a ground ball. Most squash shots are hit from a crouch and this position allows the greatest alertness.

The racket is held in a firm but not overly tight grip, its weight supported principally by the fingertips of the left hand. The purpose of cradling the racket in the left hand is to relieve the right hand of some weight and to

The ready position.

enable the left hand to help turn the body right or left as the direction of the ball dictates.

The left hand holds the racket high so that it rests in a diagonal position across the body. The purpose of this is to allow the right wrist to remain cocked all during the time the ready position is maintained. Cocking the wrist after your opponent has hit the ball may result in your making a hurried and inaccurate shot.

When the wrist is cocked, it should form a right angle with the forearm. The right arm should be slightly bent —not held high with the elbow out, since this is tiring and causes tension. The elbow of the left arm should likewise be held close to the body; balance is better and turning the body is effected more easily.

21

It is not always possible, of course, to cradle the racket in the left hand during rapid exchanges, but it should be attempted whenever possible.

PROTECTING YOURSELF

A word might be said here about another important aspect of the ready position: Its usefulness as a safeguard against being struck by your opponent's racket. In squash, as in all racket games, close watch should be kept on the ball. There are times, however, when keeping an eye on the ball involves a risk. When your opponent is hitting from behind you, it is inadvisable to turn and face him—this is dangerous and you put yourself out of position for the return—but by means of peripheral vision and turning the head somewhat, you should try to watch the ball almost until the moment of impact.

As you turn your head to keep your opponent in view, however, you should simultaneously raise your racket for protection. The most courteous opponent cannot help but come close to hitting you on some shots—particularly if you have not been alert in getting out of his way—and not all players, in their eagerness to make a winning shot, are overly concerned with the sweep of their stroke or their follow-through.

When your opponent is on your backhand side, your racket, with its head raised and cradled in your left hand, is in a good position to protect your face from a wild swing from the left. As the head and shoulders turn, the racket is brought to the left and the racket head is raised higher.

The movement is somewhat different with your opponent behind you on the right. The right hand is kept low, elbow in, and the left hand brings the racket head over to a point opposite the right shoulder at approximately eye level.

22

You should never allow your opponent to hit from *directly* behind you, since his shot will be completely hidden and there is a good chance that you will be struck by the ball—losing the point. While getting hit by the ball from behind seldom causes damage, it can be painful and cause loss of concentration.

If you see that your opponent is likely to hit from directly behind you, move to one side or the other, keeping your racket head high and turned toward his swing area for protection. From the standpoint of tactics, if you see that he is going to hit a backhand from a point directly behind you, move to his right; if he is going to hit a forehand, move to his left. He has an easy winner if he catches you between the wall and the ball.

4
The Forehand

OF ALL THE STROKES in squash, the forehand drive is probably the easiest to learn. In essence, the swing is a great deal like throwing a ball sidearm, both in the whipping action of the wrist and the placing of the feet to allow the body to impart as much power as possible. The movement of a shortstop in snapping a throw to first base is closely akin to the proper squash forehand.

The most important element in the stroking of both the forehand and backhand drives is the placement of the feet, footwork being as important in squash as it is in boxing. Of the three basic stances—open, square and closed —the one the beginner should try to assume for his ground-strokes is the closed stance. There will be many occasions, of course, when he will not have time to place himself in a closed stance—or even a square stance—but it is the ideal position from which to learn to hit proper backhands and forehands.

Adopting a closed stance insures that the racket will be drawn back in plenty of time to get set for the shot and

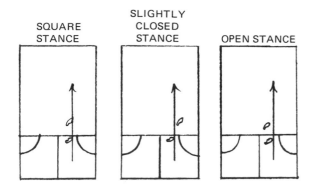

SQUARE STANCE

SLIGHTLY CLOSED STANCE

OPEN STANCE

that the body will have turned sufficiently for the most power. Not all shots are hit hard, but it is a good idea to form the habit of being prepared to hit hard as a tactical threat if nothing else.

THE CLOSED STANCE

The move into a closed stance to hit the forehand drive is accomplished in two stages:

1. From the ready position, the player (we assume he is right-handed) takes a step toward the ball with his right foot, simultaneously turning his hips and shoulders to the right so that they are parallel to the right side wall. Weight is carried mainly by the right foot.

2. The left foot now takes a step toward the ball—the size of the step depending on how near the ball will be to the player when it reaches the hitting area. It is inadvisable to take so large a step that the swing will be cramped, but it is equally important that the player not have to stretch as he swings at the ball. The left foot should point somewhat outward as the step is taken—at about a 45-degree angle to the front wall. The purpose of this is to enable the player, after making the stroke, to return easily to the ready position. The crossing movement of the left foot serves to turn the hips and shoulders farther

26

to the right. As the left foot moves past the right, forming the closed stance, weight is transferred from the right foot to the left. The greater the bend of the knees, the more pronounced the weight shift will be and the more powerful the stroke.

It is essential throughout these movements to maintain a crouch, since the most accurate drives in squash are delivered from this position. From a crouch the player can hit shots slightly above the telltale in a plane parallel to the floor—rather than in a downward plane—making it less likely that he will hit the telltale. Also, the stroke from a crouch allows the ball to be struck with a downward motion of the racket while the racket face is open—that is, tilted slightly upward. The open face imparts underspin to the ball, making it rebound downward after hitting the front wall and rising only slightly after hitting the floor. Topspin, conversely, causes the ball to rebound farther out on the floor and bounce relatively high, making an easy shot for one's opponent.

THE STROKE

Adding the racket to these movements, we find it cradled in the left hand as the step is taken by the right foot, right wrist (the main source of power) cocked as far back as possible. The racket face is open.

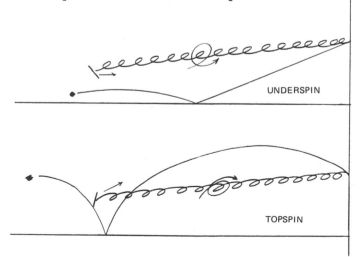

With the left hand still holding the shaft to insure the left shoulder's turning as the right foot moves, the racket is now straight up and down, the racket head about even with the right ear. The right elbow is in, the right shoulder has dropped down lower than the left and the right forearm is parallel to the floor. It is extremely important that the wrist be cocked so that it forms a right angle with the forearm.

In this position, before the completion of the backswing, there is a momentary pause. Then the left foot moves over to the right, serving to turn the hips and shoulders

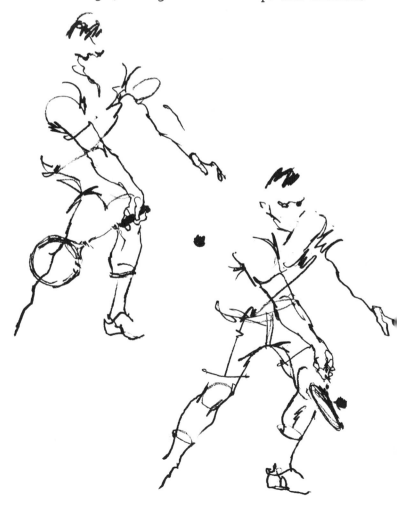

farther around, the right forearm moves back until it is nearly parallel to the side walls, the racket, because of the cocking of the wrist, remaining straight up and down. The right elbow stays tucked in. As an aid to balance, the left hand is in front of the body, palm down, looking as though it were about to catch the ball. It is considered bad manners, incidentally, to take a long backswing for the forehand—that is, extending the elbow—since one's opponent may be endangered by the flailing racket.

The racket now starts forward, hips held firm in place as long as possible. The racket face remains open. The wrist

Forehand wrist.

maintains its cocked position, the elbow stays tucked in. The forward swing starts as the racket, led by the cocked wrist, moves in a path almost parallel to the floor until the racket head reaches a point nearly opposite the left knee. At this point the wrist whips the racket head through the ball at a slightly downward angle to impart underspin. The whipping action is controlled mainly by the index finger and the thumb, and a slight pressure should be felt on these digits as the wrist makes its forward motion. Cross-court shots are hit fractionally earlier than down-the-line shots.

Along with underspin, a small amount of slice or side-spin can be imparted to the ball by drawing the strings across it from right to left. On down-the-line shots, slice keeps the ball hugging the wall, making difficult returns for one's opponent. Six inches above the telltale is the point of aim for most shots; down-the-line shots should be aimed about a foot and a half from the side wall.

After the ball is struck, the racket continues its motion

Forehand groundstroke.

in a fluid follow-through, adding pace and direction to the shot. The player finishes in a crouched position—not erect, as in tennis. In the follow-through the feeling should almost be one of throwing the racket at the wall. Finishing the stroke with the racket high in the air is another breach of courtesy, since it may endanger one's opponent. A way to make sure that the swing does not end too high is to stop the racket's forward motion with the left hand—which also serves to start the player's move into the ready position.

Once the forehand can confidently be hit with a standard backswing, the player should develop a shorter backswing as well, since very often there will not be sufficient time to pull the racket all the way back. In making the short backswing, the body turns no farther than to a position facing the side wall. Speed and power come principally from the whipping motion of the wrist as the racket meets the ball. Because the follow-through is less pronounced, assuming the ready position after the stroke can be done more quickly.

31

5
The Backhand

MOST squash players of experience would much rather take a ball on their backhand than their forehand. There are several reasons for this: The backhand can be hit with much greater speed because the ball is struck farther in front of one's body weight; it is easier to mask, or conceal, shots from the backhand side because of the delay with which the ball can be hit, and a greater variety of shots is possible because of the better view of the court the player has as he draws his racket back. All these advantages stem from the fact that in the backhand the forward arm hits the ball rather than the rear arm, as in the forehand.

In tennis, the backhand is often a bugaboo because power must be sharply controlled lest the ball sail out of the court; in squash, enclosed by walls, a player can afford to swing out without penalty. Consequently, he develops great confidence in this shot.

It is easier, too, to defend with the backhand than the forehand. That is, when a ball is hit straight at a player,

Backhand wrist.

he can poke it back with less trouble by hitting a backhand shot, the wrist and arm being already nearly in position to swing the racket.

As in the case of the forehand, the closed stance is recommended for backhand groundstrokes. From the ready position, the left foot takes a step to the left, the shoulders and hips turn left, weight is largely on the left foot. The fingertips of the left hand help support the racket as the turn begins.

The right wrist is cocked as far as possible to the left and upward, keeping the racket face open. The back of the right hand should be nearly perpendicular to the floor, while the racket shaft is held at a 45-degree angle to the floor, the racket head being at about eye level. The left elbow is tucked into the side.

There is a short pause, as with the forehand, before the right foot takes a step to the left, the weight being transferred to the right leg. As the step is taken, the hips and shoulders are drawn farther around, the right shoulder is lowered and the racket, raised by the cocked right wrist, moves far back. If the backswing is done properly, the

feeling should be that the racket is wrapped around one's neck. This is the ideal position from which to uncoil and hit a powerful shot.

As the uncoiling process begins, the wrist takes the racket forward, the right knee is sharply bent, the right elbow is tucked in, weight is on the right foot. The body is in a pronounced crouch—for power, accuracy and imparting spin.

At a point about six inches in front of the right foot, the ball is struck. The wrist whips through, the racket face is open, the racket is swung in a slightly downward path to put underspin on the ball. Again, pressure is felt on the index finger and thumb, but principally on the thumb, which supplies direction and control to the stroke. Slice, as on the forehand, can be imparted along with underspin, this time by drawing the racket strings across

the ball from left to right. For balance, the left hand is kept low and, after the forward motion starts, fairly close to the body.

The follow-through for the backhand should find the player in a crouched position—not upright. The racket face at the end of the swing should be open. The racket head should be low and the racket itself should have passed only slightly beyond an imaginary line perpendicular to the front wall. Again, the player should feel the sensation of throwing the racket at the wall as he completes the stroke. From this position, regardless of how effective he thinks the shot has been, he should quickly assume the ready position.

With the backhand (as with the forehand) it is good to develop a shorter backswing because of the speed of play. Here the body turns so that it is no more than parallel to the side wall and the racket head is brought only as

Backhand groundstroke.

high as the left shoulder, rather than past the neck. The right shoulder drops and weight is on the right leg. Wrist action supplies most of the power, and the follow-through is less pronounced than in the standard backswing, allowing the ready position to be quickly assumed.

In returning a setup with either the backhand or forehand, it is often advantageous to wait until the ball has nearly hit the floor before stroking it. The rewards of being patient in attempting putaways are that the striker can concentrate on assuming a pronounced crouch before making the shot and he has a little more time to ascertain the position of his opponent. The position of one's opponent (especially if he should commit himself) determines more than anything else the proper placement of a shot.

Backhand follow-through.

CORRECT   INCORRECT

6
The Volley

IN TOP-LEVEL tennis the volley is most often hit to win the point outright, since a ball that is angled past one's opponent cannot be retrieved. In squash, however, sharply-angled shots are likely to come off a side wall and can often be returned. Furthermore, the "get" in squash does not have to be as carefully placed as it does in tennis to stay in bounds. Scrambling for shots is a much more useful art on the squash court than the tennis court.

For these reasons, the volley in squash has not become the standard shot it has in tennis. But squash players should volley a great deal more than they do, because the volley can be a formidable weapon. Even if it does not produce outright winners, the volley is ideal for robbing an opponent of his accuracy since it permits a player to bombard his opponent with shots before he is ready to return them. Another use of the volley is to make one's opponent run for the ball without a pause for rest and before he can head for the center of the court. Squash is a game of endurance as well as skill.

Finally, the importance of the volley from a psychological standpoint cannot be overemphasized. Just as the tennis player should think in terms of hitting attacking strokes that enable him to take the net at every opportunity, so should the squash player think of moving forward in the court to take every ball possible on the volley. In addition to hurrying his opponent and forcing weak returns that can be hit for winning placements, a volleying game will tempt one's opponent to make his shots low and hard to prevent their being volleyed. In doing so, he will repeatedly hit the telltale.

FOREHAND VOLLEY

To volley in tennis, you punch the ball with a firm wrist and use very little backswing. In squash, however, the ball is not pushed back; it is hit crisply and a great deal of wrist is used. The squash player need not worry about

Forehand volley.

hitting the ball out of the court, but his shot must be hard and fast to be effective.

The key to successful volleying is the ready position. The wrist is cocked, the racket head is up, weight is forward—enabling the player to meet the ball quickly and in front of his body.

As the ball approaches, the right foot moves to the right as for the forehand drive. The shoulders, however, do not turn all the way back but make a half right angle to the front wall. As the shoulders turn, the right shoulder lowers and the right wrist turns to the right, causing the racket face to open. The left hand leaves the racket sooner than it does for the forehand groundstroke, with the racket taken back only slightly beyond the right shoulder. Because of lack of time to make this shot, the backswing is necessarily short.

A short, quick step to the right is now taken by the left foot, allowing the player to hit the ball from an open stance. Weight is transferred to the left foot, knees are bent, the body leans forward. As the step is taken with the left foot, the forward movement of the racket is begun, enabling it to meet the ball sooner than in the forehand groundstroke. There is also more of a sense of forward movement on the part of the body as the forehand volley is hit, since this is an aggressive, attacking shot.

Throughout the stroke, the right elbow should stay close to the body and the racket head should remain higher than the wrist. If a low ball is to be volleyed, the player should get down to it by bending his knees, not by dropping the racket head.

The wrist leads the racket face into the ball, snapping across it in a slightly downward motion to impart backspin and sidespin, the index finger and thumb supplying most of the power. The left hand is raised and placed forward for balance. The follow-through is not as full as for the groundstroke, although the feeling should be, again, one of throwing the racket at the front wall. It is important at the finish of the stroke to be ready for a fast

Backhand volley.

return—especially one that can be hit for a winner—hence keeping one's balance is essential.

BACKHAND VOLLEY

The backhand volley is easier to prepare for than the forehand, since the racket is almost in position to stroke it as the opponent's return is being made. Preparatory movements for the shot are like those for the forehand volley, but reversed.

The left foot is moved toward the left side wall, the shoulders are twisted in a quarter turn to the left and the left wrist is turned as far left as possible to open the racket face. The right shoulder is lowered and the backswing is short—the racket being taken no farther back than the left shoulder. (See below.)

As the right foot takes a short, quick step to form an open stance, the forward movement of the racket begins, the body in a pronounced forward lean, right elbow tucked in. The wrist brings the racket forward with an open face

and snaps the racket head through the ball in a slightly downward motion. Again, the racket head stays higher than the wrist. As in the case of the forehand volley, the ball on the backhand volley is taken farther in front of the body than it is on the groundstroke. The left arm hangs almost vertically as the stroke is made.

TYPES OF VOLLEYS

The beginner will find that he is most successful in volleying cross court, since his body will be behind his shots and there will be less tendency to crowd the ball. Once mastery of the cross-court volley is attained, down-the-line volleys should be attempted. On this shot, the ball is hit later and with faster wrist action.

It is inadvisable to attempt to change the plane of the ball's flight in volleying. That is, if the ball comes at the player at waist height, his return should be aimed to hit the wall at waist height, not lower. A ball coming low off the wall should be returned low. Pinpoint accuracy in volleying is not as important as hitting the ball solidly and crisply. The purpose of this stroke is to get the ball back fast, rushing one's opponent. Risking an error for the sake of a possible putaway is not good tactics.

If, during a rally, the player is in a position to volley and the ball comes off the front wall at a height greater than his shoulder, he is advised to let it go, turn and get into position to take it off the back wall. Stroking a firm volley at this height is quite difficult, whereas a ball coming off the back wall at fair speed presents an opportunity for an easy winner.

THE HALF-VOLLEY

Hitting a half-volley—returning the ball immediately after it bounces—can be both an offensive and defensive shot. Sometimes a player has no choice but to half-volley a ball—

it is the only way the ball can be played—and the stroke is defensive. On the other hand, an aggressive player can utilize the half-volley in much the same way he uses the volley. It is a tactical shot used to hurry an opponent's return or to tire him out.

In either case, there are good ways and bad ones to hit the half-volley. The ball should always be hit out in front of the body, the weight moving forward, not leaning back. If the weight is not moving forward on the stroke, the ball is likely to be popped up in the air, presenting a setup for one's opponent. It is important to get the right shoulder down when hitting a half-volley so the ball can be directed more accurately. Half-volleys should be aimed higher than groundstrokes, since they are more difficult to place accurately in relation to the telltale. Ideally, they should be hit with the racket head higher than the wrist, but often, particularly on defensive half-volleys, this is not possible.

To be effective, backhand volleys should be hit earlier than forehand volleys and for this reason the backhand half-volley is considered the more difficult of the two shots.

Finally, the player should not be afraid of hitting half-volleys as an aggressive tactic. Even though the ball may not go exactly where intended, consistent use of the stroke is likely to hurry the shots of one's opponent to the point where his accuracy will suffer and his confidence will be shaken.

7
The Service

THE SERVE in squash is not the decisive weapon it often is in tennis, where the receiver can either be aced or forced to hit such a weak return that the server scores a quick point. On the other hand, the squash service is not merely a haphazard stroke to put the ball in play.

The lob service—the most useful of squash serves despite the fact that it falls slowly and looks easy to return—can be very effective in forcing weak replies. Both the slice serve and the hard serve, when used conservatively, can cramp an opponent's return so that he will be kept on the defensive until the server hits an eventual putaway. Both of these serves occasionally produce outright winners, especially against a weary opponent.

Perhaps the biggest difference between the serve in tennis and that in squash is that the tennis receiver is usually defensive-minded, wondering how he can get the ball past the onrushing server, whereas the receiver in squash is offensive-minded, hoping the server will send him a setup that he can volley for a placement. Partly accounting for this difference in attitude is the fact that in tennis the receiver is not allowed to volley the serve, while there is no such restriction in squash. Indeed, the squash player who does not volley the service return usually finds himself in deep trouble.

THE LOB SERVE

For several reasons, this is the most popular serve in squash. It takes very little energy to hit, the server is given time to move into the T position and he is not off balance after hitting the ball. (A hard or sliced serve sometimes throws the server off balance.) Finally, the server, if he is skillful, knows almost exactly where the ball will land, or where it must be taken if volleyed; the hard server or slice server cannot always be sure of the precise direction and depth of the ball. As in all serves, the right-handed player hits the lob serve from his forehand side in each service box, using the Continental grip. (It is inadvisable to hit serves from one's backhand side.)

To serve the lob to a receiver standing in the left-hand court, the server places his right foot in the service box, or quarter circle, on the right. The right foot should be in that part of the quarter circle nearest the center of the court and should point toward the right side wall. The left foot is outside the quarter circle and in front of the floor service line. It points slightly forward. The feet are about shoulder width apart. The stance is slightly open, shoulders are approximately parallel to the right side wall. Weight is on the right leg. If either foot touches the quarter circle lines, the server has committed a foot-fault and the serve is considered a fault.

The server stands erect, racket cradled in the left hand, as in the ready position. The ball is also held in the left hand. After seeing that the receiver is ready, he looks at the spot on the front wall he wants to hit—the ideal spot

48

Lob serve.

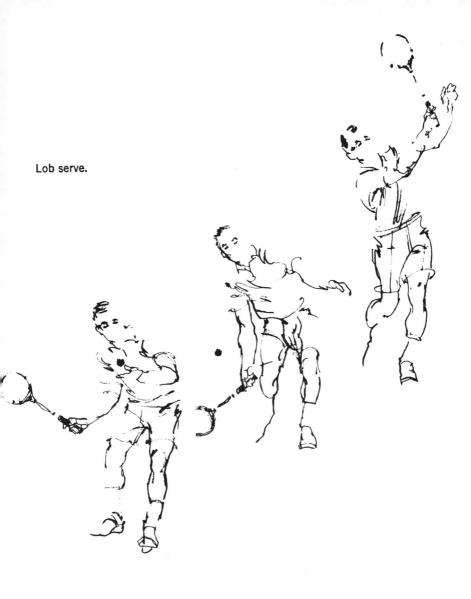

is just to the left of center and almost at the top of the wall.

With the knees bent so that the body is in a crouch, the racket is released by the left hand and lowered. There is very little backswing. The left hand reaches forward and drops the ball. As it falls it is met by the upward-moving racket and lifted up toward the front wall. The racket face should be open, adding—in this case—topspin to the ball. Topspin gives the ball extra height as it comes off the front wall.

After the ball is lofted, the server, eye on the ball as it hits the wall and comes down, takes his position in the T, ready to play the return. If the ball hits fairly far back in the receiver's court, the server should follow its flight by means of peripheral vision. If it lands close to the center line, he should remember to give the receiver all the room he needs to play his shot.

To serve to a player in the right-hand court, the server's right foot is placed in the quarter circle on the left as near to the center of the court as possible. The right foot points toward the right side wall. The left foot, outside the quarter circle and in front of the floor service line, points approximately in the direction of the front wall. The stance is slightly closed. The ball in this case is hit just to the right of the center of the front wall and quite close to the top.

The most effective lob serve comes off the front wall with very little speed and glances off the side wall while traveling in an almost vertical trajectory. A serve that glances off the side wall just behind the service line, forcing the receiver to decide quickly whether to volley the ball just before it hits the wall, take it on the bounce or off the back wall, is very difficult to return. In either case, the receiver will be hitting a ball dropping almost vertically at a point somewhere over his head, with the side wall restricting free movement of his racket. He must hit the ball while standing erect, relying almost solely on his wrist for power and direction. On the backhand especially, this is a frequent point winner for the server.

Careless hitting of the lob serve, however, gives the receiver a chance to put the server on the defensive or win the point outright. A typical poor lob serve is one that does not glance off the side wall, allowing an easy volley. Another is a serve that comes off the front wall at a low angle—again an easy volley for the receiver.

Finally, there are the serves that come off the front wall so fast that they hit the back wall, or the back and side walls, before bouncing on the floor. All these are dangerous for the server from a tactical standpoint. The receiver, instead of volleying, lets the ball hit the rear wall and follows it as it breaks out toward the middle of the court. Either by "turning on the ball" (generally done on the backhand side) or "backing on the ball" (done on both sides but most often on the forehand), the receiver can force the server completely out of position.

The receiver is allowed to hit the ball as late as he wishes and the server must make room for him, no matter how inconvenient, so that the return can be made. Consequently, a wily receiver can so time his service return that by the time he hits the ball, the server is completely blocked out of the play.

An ideal lob service, on the other hand, is one that is hit just deep enough, if not taken on the volley, to bounce on the floor at the rear of the service court quite close to the back wall. Because the ball rebounds only a few inches off the back wall, the receiver is confronted with a most difficult return.

THE HARD SERVE

Although this serve—which can be likened to the cannonball in tennis—may win points in a spectacular way, it should be used sparingly. If it is hit too frequently, the receiver will become used to its speed and take advantage

51

of the server's being momentarily off balance after he hits it—particularly from the left-hand service box. Besides that, the serve is extremely tiring when kept up through a series of games.

The preparatory position for the hard serve is exactly the same as for the lob serve, primarily for the purpose of deception. The first indication to the receiver that the hard serve is to be hit may be the upward toss of the ball by the server's left hand. The ball should be tossed so that it can be hit above the right shoulder, the racket action being similar to hammering a nail.

With the wrist cocked, the racket is drawn straight back over the right shoulder. Then, at the top of the ball's trajectory, it is brought forward in a throwing motion. Breaking the wrist as the ball is hit adds power to the shot. The ball should be hit flat, not with a slice, and it

Hard serve.

should be aimed low—as close to the front wall service line as possible.

The hard service has several functions: It acts as a change of pace to keep an opponent off balance; it is useful against an opponent who is perplexed by its speed; and, finally, it may be a point winner after a long, tiring rally, when the receiver's reflexes have slowed down.

The hard serve can be hit to various parts of the receiver's court. Possibly the safest hard serve is one aimed to come off the front wall directly at the receiver. If it is hit properly, the receiver will not be able to do more than poke it back, giving the server a chance for a winner. The serve should be hit hard enough so that, should the receiver let it go, it will hit the back wall before bouncing on the floor. If the serve happens to bounce before hitting the back wall, the receiver, because of the ball's reduced speed as it comes off the wall, will have an easy shot.

The hard serve can also be aimed to hit the back corners of the two service courts. It is important, however, not to hit the side wall in the service-court area with this cross-

court serve, since the receiver can then turn on the ball or back on the ball, obtaining a tactical advantage as he forces the server out of position. The service should be hit hard enough to strike the back wall before bouncing.

A third, and relatively tricky, hard serve is one that strikes the front wall very close to the side wall and comes back to the receiver at an unusual angle. From the right-hand service box, the ball, after hitting the left side of the front wall, rebounds to the left side wall and heads directly toward the receiver at considerable speed. Ideally, if the receiver fails to take the ball on the volley, the ball

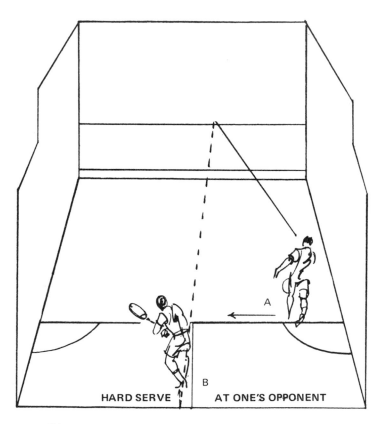

HARD SERVE AT ONE'S OPPONENT

should bounce in the forward right-hand corner of the left service court. From here, it shoots to the back wall with so much speed and spin that it is virtually impossible to return. The receiver is best off if he takes this serve on the volley—but the unusual direction from which it approaches often causes temporary confusion and forces the receiver to make a weak return. From the left-hand service box the ball's flight is of course reversed. It hits the right side of the front wall, rebounds off the right side wall and bounces in the forward left-hand corner of the right service court. (See page 56.)

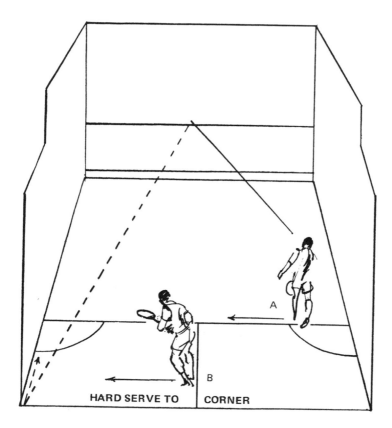

HARD SERVE TO CORNER

This serve contains an element of bluff, inasmuch as the receiver, not daring to let the ball bounce and skitter away from him, will volley many serves that conceivably might have been faults.

A final hard serve—not recommended unless the server has great speed—is one that, from the right service box, hits the front wall low and left of center, rebounding at nearly a right angle to a point slightly past the middle of the side wall and from there crosses the left quarter circle and hits the back wall in the approximate center of the

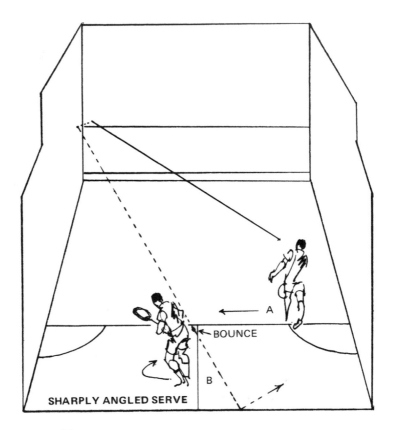

A

← BOUNCE

B

SHARPLY ANGLED SERVE

left service court. Again, the unusual angle at which the ball approaches the receiver may force him to hit a weak volley. On the other hand, if the receiver can handle the server's speed, the ball is in the open for a volleyed placement; or, having decided not to volley, the receiver may be able to turn on the ball and have an easy shot.

The hard service should be relied on more than usual in courts in which the temperature is high, when the ball seems especially lively or when the ceiling is so low that the lob service cannot be used effectively.

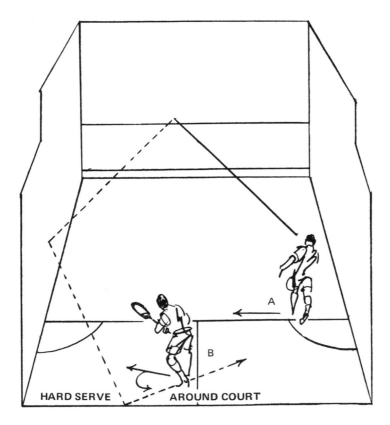

Slice serve.

THE SLICE SERVE

For the purpose of deception, the same preparatory position is adopted for the slice serve as for the others. As the left hand tosses the ball up and to the right, the racket is taken back to the side, with the racket head coming to about shoulder height. The ball is struck on its downward trajectory slightly above shoulder height with a somewhat sideward swing. The racket face is open and

58

the strings, instead of hitting the ball flat, are drawn sharply across the ball from right to left, imparting a great deal of sidespin.

A ball served from the right quarter circle should hit just above the front wall service line and slightly to the left of center; one served from the left quarter circle should hit the front wall at the same height and slightly to the right of center. The spin imparted causes the serve to rebound from the front wall at a sharp downward angle.

Coming off the wall, the slice serve most difficult to return by a receiver standing in the right service court strikes low on the right side wall just beyond the floor service line and hits the floor almost simultaneously. For a receiver in the left service court, the ball should strike low on the left side wall just beyond the service line and immediately hit the floor. The serve should not be hit so hard that it reaches the back wall after bouncing. Once again the receiver can place the server at a tactical disadvantage by playing the ball off the back wall. The height at which the serve hits the side wall should be varied occasionally to keep the receiver off balance.

Like the hard serve, the slice is useful in courts with low ceilings and when a change of pace is advisable. If the receiver handles one's lob service easily, the slice serve should be employed.

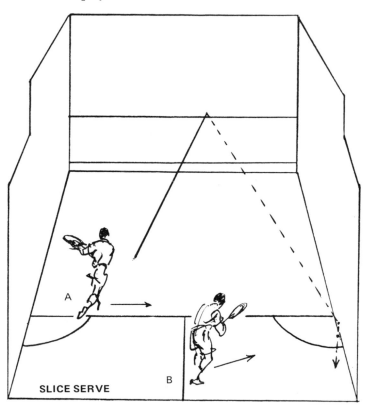

SLICE SERVE

8
The Return of Service

JUST as the server must be studiously careful about where he places his serve, so must the receiver be with his return. Many points are lost because the receiver overestimated his ability to kill a slow-moving serve; and many more are lost because the receiver, in failing to volley the serve, left himself a difficult shot which allowed the server, anchored in the center of the court, to control the play.

All three of the basic serves—lob, slice and hard serve —should be awaited in the same manner: The receiver faces the side wall adjoining the court he is receiving in, feet just inside the center line, his head turned toward the server. If the server stands in the right-hand quarter circle, the receiver faces the left side wall; if the server stands in the left-hand quarter circle, the receiver faces the right side wall. He should be about three feet away from the back wall, giving himself room to swing the racket. The ready position is assumed, with this difference: In the left court, the receiver expects to take the ball on his backhand; in the right court, he expects to take it on his forehand. Like a batter in baseball wisely setting himself for a fast ball, the receiver in squash should always be ready for the hard serve.

LOB SERVE RETURN IN THE LEFT COURT

To return a lob serve in the left court, the receiver steps toward the center of the court with his left foot as he judges precisely where the ball will be taken. The racket is brought a short way back as the shoulders turn and the right foot takes a step toward the left side wall. The ball should be volleyed—hit in front of the body. If the serve is well-placed, the position of the receiver will probably be erect and power must be imparted to the return with a wrist snap.

The best return is a rail shot hitting about two feet above the front wall service line. The ball should not at any time hit the side wall and, on returning from the front

Backhand return of lob serve.

Forehand return of lob serve.

wall, should bounce close to the floor service line. The return must not be too high, or the server will have an easy volley. The cross-court return of this serve (the second most effective return) should hit about two feet above the tin.

LOB SERVE RETURN IN THE RIGHT COURT

The receiver faces the right wall; eyes on the server, ready to hit a forehand. When the ball is hit, he judges its speed and direction, moves toward the right side wall with his right foot, steps over with the left and, with his weight on the left foot, volleys on his forehand. The serve is much easier to return on this side and should be aimed, in most cases, down the line. In the right court especially, the receiver looks for a poor serve that will give him a chance to hit a winner or a shot that will enable him to wrest the T from the server.

RETURNING A LOB SERVE THAT COMES OUT

A lob serve that comes out is one that has been hit too hard and travels directly from the front wall to the back wall, or from the front wall to a side wall and the back wall, before hitting the floor.

The receiver has a choice of two ways to play the return if he decides to let the ball come out. He may "back on the ball" or "turn on the ball." In the left service court, both methods are used by the right-handed player. In backing on the ball, he takes it on his backhand; in turning on the ball, he takes it on his forehand. The right-handed player seldom turns on the ball in the right service court; he is much more apt to back on it, hitting it with his forehand.

Backing on a lob serve in the left-hand court consists of making ready to hit a backhand and carefully gauging the flight of the ball to see how far out on the floor it will break after hitting the back wall. The receiver should not move back with the ball but should be ready to move down court as quickly as possible, since the ball will come off the wall quite rapidly. The wrist is cocked, right shoulder is lowered and the player must make sure to stay away from the ball—not allow it to come too close to his body. For power, the player should quickly shift his weight from the rear foot to the front foot as he swings. From a tactical standpoint, the farther forward the receiver can move in the court and the longer he can delay

Backing on the ball—backhand.

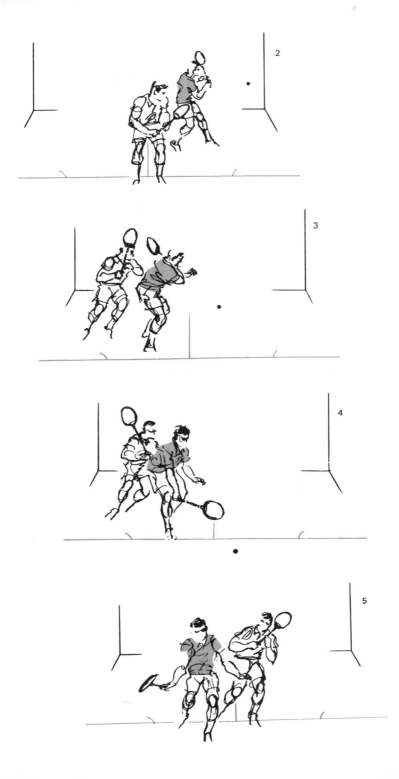

his swing, the more he will force the server out of position. A rail shot, with the server boxed out of the play, is a sure winner.

To back on a ball served in the right-hand court, the receiver gauges the flight of the ball, draws his racket back for a forehand, stays away from the ball and again hits it as late and as far down-court as possible to force the server out of position. Weight is on the left foot to impart the greatest power to the shot. Again, a rail shot—this time along the right side wall—should win the point.

Rail shots in this tactical position should not be hit so hard or so high, however, that they rebound all the way to the rear wall. If they do, one's opponent has a clear path to the ball and time to retrieve it. Rail shots should be hit for "length"—that is, aimed to strike the front wall at a height and speed that allows them to bounce twice before reaching the back wall. A rail shot hit hard from a point near the front wall must be aimed fairly low and should carry underspin and sidespin to bring the ball to the floor quickly; a rail shot that will hit the front wall fairly high should be stroked with less force.

In tactical situations like these—when a putaway or forcing shot can be made—it is usually advisable to hit the ball away from one's opponent, as opposed to trying to outguess him by hitting the ball to the spot he has just vacated or is about to vacate. This is a mistake made by experts as well as beginners. Even if your opponent anticipates the direction of the shot and arrives in time to make

Backing on the ball—forehand.

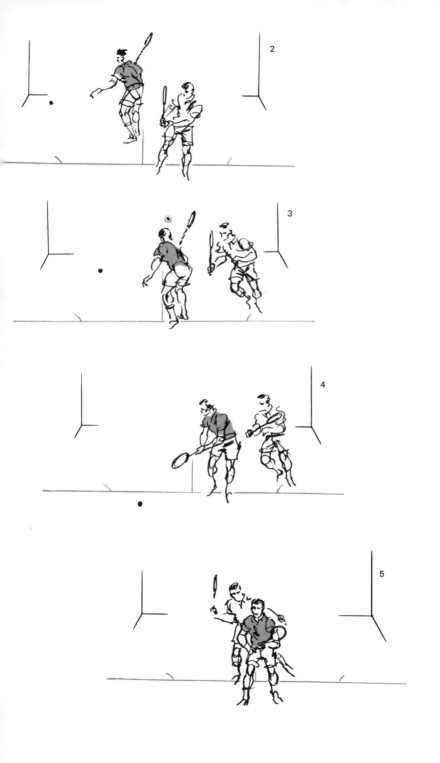

a return, you will have made him move about the court, thus contributing to his fatigue. Only occasionally—after several instances of hitting away from your opponent—should you attempt to catch him running in the wrong direction.

Turning on a ball received in the left court consists of carefully gauging the ball's speed and direction and pivoting to the left as the racket is drawn back to hit a forehand. As the receiver pivots, he calls, "Turning!" to warn the server that his swing will come from the forehand, rather than the backhand, side. As with the backing procedures, the receiver can force the server out of position as he pursues the ball. A well-hit rail shot, after turning on the ball in the left service court, is almost a sure point for the receiver.

In cases where the ball hits the floor before it hits the back wall—either during a rally or on the serve—it will come off the back wall much more slowly, presenting, with practice, a relatively easy shot even though it must be made in the backcourt area. The player's racket should be kept fairly close to the ball as he moves back. The racket face should be open and the player should be, at the closest, fully three feet away from the back wall to avoid cramping his shot. Again, power is imparted to the stroke principally by a quick weight shift from the rear foot to the forward one as the ball is hit.

Turning on the ball—forehand.

2

3

4

5

RETURNING A HARD SERVE

All hard serves, regardless of angle or speed, should be volleyed. The receiver should be aware, while awaiting a possible hard serve, that he will not have time to take a standard backswing but must block the ball with his racket. Wrist very firm, he relies on the serve's own speed to carry the ball back to the front wall. Since the server is likely to be off balance after serving, it is possible he will have some trouble with a ball returned straight at him, making the cross-court return the most effective shot. It is important not to panic against a hard server; this increases his confidence. The first few times the receiver tries to return a hard serve he may be perplexed; but soon he should be able to time it accurately and his blocked returns will place the server in difficulty.

The hard serve hit from the right-hand quarter circle which strikes the left side of the front wall, rebounds against the left side wall and comes at the receiver diagonally is best taken on the forehand, though the receiver must move very quickly to get into position. The open stance is recommended in making this shot. The return should be aimed at the front wall so that it rebounds to the rear corner on the left, making the server run the greatest distance possible.

A hard serve hit from the left quarter circle which strikes the front wall, rebounds off the right side wall and heads for the receiver diagonally on his right should be taken on the backhand. The return should be aimed for the rear right-hand corner of the court.

RETURN OF THE SLICE SERVE

It is almost imperative that this serve, which bounces low against the wall, be returned on the volley. The receiver must move forward quickly and bend low to get to the ball before it strikes the side wall. The most effective return—whether the serve is taken on the volley or after it bounces—is cross-court.

On his return of service, the beginning player should have two objectives: Hitting a return that is not slowed down by glancing off the side walls, and hitting a return that moves the server slightly out of position so that the T position may be taken.

9
Tactics

CONTROL of the center of the court—the closest point to all possible returns—is the key to achieving the two basic aims in squash: Forcing one's opponent to make weak returns that can be hit for winners, and moving him about the court so rapidly that fatigue will impair his accuracy. The main tactical battle, then, becomes a heated contest for possession of the T.

The best shots from backcourt are those which make one's opponent abandon the T; the worst are those which he can return while remaining in the vicinity of the T. Rail shots and cross-courts—hit hard but not necessarily low—are the basic shots used to drive one's opponent from the center. A high lob, hit deep and parallel to the side wall, is also effective.

Beginners often make the following mistakes in backcourt tactics:

• Trying to hit balls low off the front wall for winners and hitting the telltale instead

- Hitting shots that strike the side wall before reaching the front wall, allowing one's opponent to stroke winners from the center of the court
- Failing to move in and volley a shot when the opportunity arises, thus missing a chance to capture the center

Once the center is gained, shots should be directed toward keeping one's opponent off balance and moving him as far out of position as possible. The kind of shot used—rail, cross-court, drop, corner or reverse corner—is determined by the position of one's opponent. Even if, through fine anticipation, he returns one or more of these shots, sooner or later the court will be opened up for an irretrievable placement. Often when one's opponent cannot be seen, his position can be ascertained by the sounds he makes with his feet.

In playing against a hard hitter, it is best to keep him back in the corners rather than try to outslug him. Against a slow-moving but experienced player, shots should be kept low, with volleys and half-volleys frequently used. Returns against the retrieving type of player should force him to do a great deal of running, while patience must be kept when he persistently gets back shots that would ordinarily be winners.

Finally, it is important to remember that everyone who takes part in competitive sports makes mistakes. The players who achieve the greatest success are those who do not brood over their errors but profit by them.

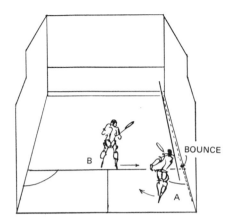

RAIL SHOT FROM BACKCOURT

Winners are not often hit from the backcourt area when one's opponent is alertly posted in the T. Player A's main concern should be to dislodge B from the T so that he can place himself there. His basic tactics are to hit shots close to the side walls so that B will have to move to one side or the other. As B moves, A heads for the T—in most cases circling behind B so as not to interfere with B's return.

One of the three basic ways to take the T is to hit a rail shot not too low and with good pace so that it will have length. The ball, on rebounding from the front wall, should bounce near the floor service line. B is given the choice of playing a difficult volley or moving to the back of the court to hit a groundstroke, leaving the T position open. If the shot is hit too high, however, B's volley is easier; if the shot is too low, B can take it after it bounces in the forecourt and perhaps score a winner.

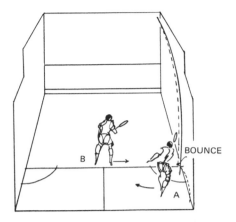

HIGH LOB FROM BACKCOURT

The second basic shot from backcourt is the high lob. The ball should not hit the side wall either going up or coming down and, ideally, should bounce at about the floor service line. It is a shot that should be practiced a good deal before being utilized in a game, since if it comes short off the front wall, one's opponent has an easy volley. The stroke is made from a more erect position than the drive and the swing resembles that used for the lob serve. If hit correctly, the lob allows the player ample time to take possession of the T.

CROSS-COURT SHOT FROM BACKCOURT

In hitting the cross-court shot from the back of the court, a winner should not be attempted nor should the ball be hit too low. Player A hits the ball hard, moving forward with the stroke, adding power to it. As B moves to take the ball, A heads for the T. The ball should hit low on the opposite side wall and bounce close to the floor

76

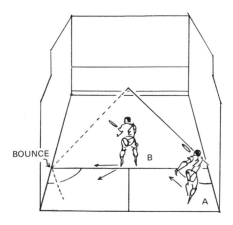

service line. B has a choice of hitting a difficult backhand volley or, having let the ball bounce, turning on it and trying to catch up with it to hit a forehand after the ball has come off the back wall. In either case, he has abandoned the T. Player A must be careful to hit the front wall in the approximate center, or Player B, moving forward, has a chance to make a placement. (See above.)

BOAST FOR NICK FROM BACKCOURT

Though the boast for nick from the backcourt area looks like a desperation shot, it is becoming more and more popular each year as a possible point winner. In the past

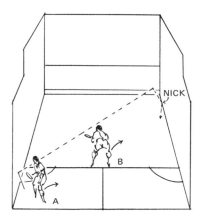

the boast—a return hit hard at the nearer side wall so that it rebounds to the front wall near the corner—was primarily a defensive shot, the player being confronted with a ball on his backhand (or forehand) that he could not hit straight toward the front wall; now it is used as an offensive shot, provided the player has an "on" day. The shot (primarily taken on the backhand side because of the power that can be put into the stroke) is hit hard and up into the side wall. The stance is extremely closed, with weight firmly on the forward foot. Even if the shot does not nick after hitting the front wall, one's opponent has a difficult shot in the forecourt. (See diagram at bottom of page 77.)

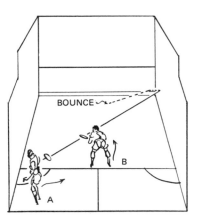

REVERSE CORNER SHOT FROM BACKCOURT

From the backcourt area, the reverse corner shot (or cross-court corner shot) is an extremely risky one, involving extreme accuracy and delicate touch. If the ball hits the side wall too far back, or if the shot hits the front wall first, Player B can pounce on the ball for an easy winner. After playing the shot, A should quickly move to the T position to be ready for B's return. (See above.)

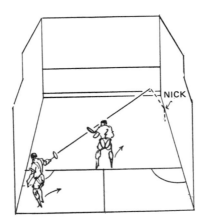

CROSS-COURT DROP SHOT FROM BACKCOURT

Like the reverse corner shot, the cross-court drop shot from backcourt requires extremely delicate touch. It is a valuable shot to add to one's repertory and is becoming more popular than the reverse corner shot, which leaves the ball in the center of the court. Even if not hit perfectly, the cross-court drop, like the backcourt boast for nick, leaves one's opponent with a difficult shot near the forecourt wall.

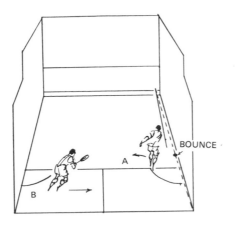

RAIL SHOT FROM MIDCOURT

Permitted to advance to the midcourt area, Player A now has a greater opportunity to hit for winners. This does not mean that shots should be played leaving no margin for error, but A can hit the ball harder and lower, giving B more difficult shots to return. A can also reach the T position by moving forward, rather than circling back as was the case after hitting shots from backcourt. With B in the position shown, A's best tactic is a rail shot.

CROSS-COURT SHOT FROM MIDCOURT

As in the previous position, A has a chance to hit a clean winner—this time with a cross-court. He should drive the ball low—so that it hits about six inches above the tin—and try to make it strike the side wall at a point nearly opposite Player B. A should mask his shot as much as possible.

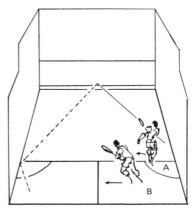

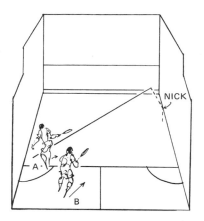

CROSS-COURT DROP SHOT FROM MIDCOURT

From the midcourt area the cross-court drop shot is not as risky as it is from backcourt. The shot does not have to be played with pinpoint accuracy and A is better able to mask the direction and speed of his shot, since B is behind him, rather than in front of him. It is inadvisable, however, for A to overexaggerate his backswing for purposes of deception, since B may then guess his intention.

REVERSE CORNER SHOT FROM MIDCOURT

With Player B in the rear of the court and on the opposite side, the reverse corner shot (or cross-court corner shot) can be a point winner from midcourt. It is advisable to stroke this shot crisply, not slowly, the way a corner shot or a drop shot is hit. A slowly hit ball in this situation gives B an easy shot in the forecourt.

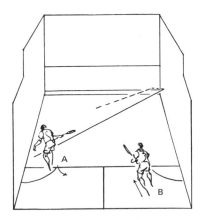

CORNER SHOT FROM MIDCOURT

When Player B is caught out of position, as shown, and A is in midcourt, a corner shot, crisply hit, makes a difficult return for B. A great deal of slice should be imparted to the ball so that, after hitting the side wall, it will die quickly off the front wall. After making the shot, A must move quickly out of B's way or B may run into him, causing a let.

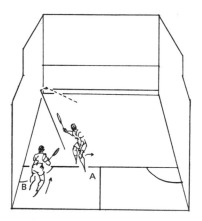

RAIL SHOT IN THE FORECOURT

When a player is given the opportunity to hit the ball from positions near the front wall, he has his choice of a variety of offensive shots. All shots in this area, except for difficult retrieves, should be played for winners. The position of one's opponent determines how hard and in what direction the ball should be hit.

Having gotten his feet around properly, Player A here

82

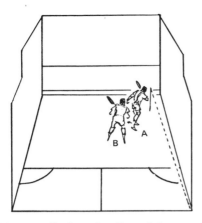

hits a rail shot hard and low, taking advantage of Player B's advance forward from the T. B's advance is not considered sound tactics and he will have a difficult time retrieving A's shot. (See above.)

CROSS-COURT SHOT IN THE FORECOURT

The easiest shot played from close to the front wall is the cross-court. It can be hit harder than the rail shot and its eventual direction can be masked a split-second longer if skillfully executed. Again, B's tendency to advance from the T is taken advantage of. A ball breaking off the side wall, as shown, will be difficult for B to get. Player A should not overwork the cross-court or his opponent will come to anticipate it.

After hitting a shot in the forecourt, the player, if he returns to the T, should not turn and face the rear wall but should back up into position.

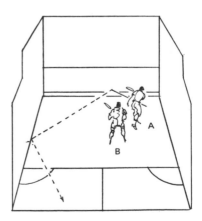

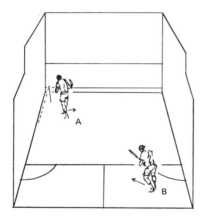

DROP SHOT IN THE FORECOURT

The forecourt drop shot, hit with a flick of the wrist, is not an auxiliary shot, as when hit from backcourt and midcourt areas, but is a sure winner when set up properly. Hitting hard low drives from the forecourt which keep one's opponent well back is the best way to set up the drop shot. Even if B, anticipating the shot, should reach the ball, he has a difficult return. The ball will bounce close to the wall and A is in a good position to put away B's lunging retrieve. The grip should not be loosened for the drop shot or the ball may not reach the wall.

CORNER SHOT IN THE FORECOURT

With Player B in the rear of the court, Player A hits a backhand corner shot off the side wall nearest his opponent. This shot, as all shots, should be approached as though it were going to be stroked hard; then Player A rolls it softly around the corner, imparting little underspin but a great deal of slice. The ball will come quickly off the side wall and, after hitting the front wall, will tend to rebound from it in a nearly parallel direction.

If Players B and A were on the right side of the court, A's sliced corner shot, played on his forehand, would first hit the right side wall.

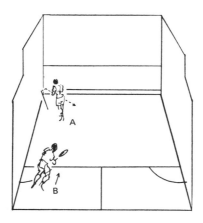

PHILADELPHIA BOAST

Player A here plays a tricky shot—the Philadelphia Boast —a kind of boast in reverse, hit only from the forecourt. The ball is struck so that it bounces high off the front wall to the side wall, picking up a great deal of reverse spin. It then comes diagonally across the court to hit the opposite side wall and, because of the spin, rebounds almost perpendicularly. On reaching the back wall, if allowed to travel that far, the ball rebounds parallel to it—an impossible shot to retrieve. Player B's best return of the shot is a volley, which puts A in danger of being hit in the head. A, therefore, should be very careful to get out of B's way after making this shot.

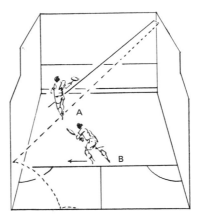

10
Practice

BECAUSE the ball almost always comes back, squash is the ideal game for practicing various shots, but time spent practicing is not always used effectively. The player should not return the ball to the front wall aimlessly; he should isolate each type of shot and practice each one individually for a definite period of time. In particular he should practice those shots he is least sure of.

About twenty-five minutes is sufficient time for a hard practice workout. A tentative schedule might be:

3 minutes of short-swing forehands
3 minutes of standard forehands
3 minutes of short-swing backhands
3 minutes of standard backhands
3 minutes of alternating forehands and backhands
4 minutes of serves (a breather)
2 minutes of forehand volleys
2 minutes of backhand volleys
2 minutes of alternating forehand and backhand volleys

Improvement will come much more quickly if the player, after practice, limits his games to three than if he forgoes practice and plays, say, six games. In the fifth or sixth game his concentration is bound to lapse and fatigue may make him develop lazy, improper stroking habits. It is also unwise to depend solely on playing the game to develop endurance and speed afoot. Attainment of these qualities is hastened by long-distance running, skipping rope and wind sprints.

A final note: It is extremely important to be thoroughly warmed up before playing a match. The room is usually cold—from 35 to 45 degrees—and while a player's arm may get quickly warmed up, it does not follow that his body and legs will do the same. The player should not only hit a good many shots by himself prior to play (preferably in the court to be used) but should also do light calisthenics. Because of the quick, sudden moves required in squash, failure to warm up properly can result in strained muscles and ligaments. Moreover, proper warmup allows the player to play hard from the very beginning of a match instead of sloughing away points while waiting for the body and legs to catch up with the arm. Points won at the beginning of a match count just as much as those won later on.

PRACTICING THE SHORT SWING

Practicing groundstrokes is most systematically done by taking a position near the side wall (right for forehand, left for backhand) and at first hitting the ball with a shortened swing, the racket being drawn only about halfway back. The feet are in a slightly closed stance and placed just behind the service line, which is used as a point of reference. The racket is held at knee height, face open, shaft parallel to the floor, racket head pointing toward the right wall. Elbow is tucked in. (As a disciplinary measure it might be advisable to place a squash ball under the top

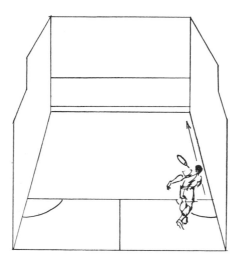

part of the arm, between the biceps and the body, making sure that it does not fall to the floor until the stroke is completed.)

The left hand tosses the ball (a different one) against the side wall so that when it rebounds it bounces at a point approximately opposite the left foot—the point at which the ball can be hit with maximum power. As the ball is released, the racket is drawn back, the weight moves forward and the wrist whips the racket through the ball. The ball should be hit parallel to the side wall and should strike the front wall about four inches above the telltale. After each shot, the ball is retrieved and the exercise is repeated. Besides improving wrist action and helping the player learn racket control, the exercise helps the player determine where the ball should be hit, in relation to his body, for hard, accurate rail shots.

Once the rhythm of the short swing is attained, the player should move back a few feet to the center of the service box, maintaining the same distance from the side wall, and again face the wall in a slightly closed stance.

The racket is held in the same position as the ball is

tossed against the wall, but is drawn back this time in a full backswing. The ball, after being tossed up against the wall as before, is hit quite hard. The ball is aimed four inches above the telltale and parallel to the side wall, but this time the same forehand stroke is repeated as the ball rebounds off the front wall, feet remaining in the same position. Once the practice rail shot is perfected, the ball can be hit as many as 30 times in succession without changing the position of the feet.

In practicing the short swing and standard swing with the backhand, the ball is tossed against the left side wall so that it bounces in front of the right foot.

EXERCISE FOR RACKET CONTROL

To increase racket control in the groundstrokes, the player should stand facing the front wall, heels close to the floor service line, and hit alternate backhands and forehands, remembering to crouch with each stroke, and keep the ball in play as long as possible. The feet are not moved.

After mastery of the exercise from this position in the court is attained, the player takes a new position closer to the front wall, requiring quicker racket action, quicker reflexes and faster body movement.

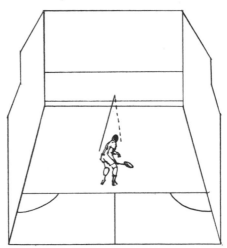

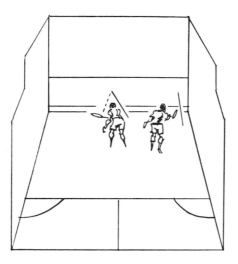

VOLLEY PRACTICE

There are two methods of practicing the volley. In the first, the player stands in the forecourt facing the side wall, feet in an open stance, and tries to volley as many forehands as possible without changing the position of his feet. Then he turns and volleys as many backhands as possible. The exercise helps the player to learn racket control and the timing of the volley. As he becomes more proficient, he stations himself farther forward in the court.

The second method, requiring fine timing and racket control, consists of the player's facing the front wall in the middle of the forecourt and volleying from his backhand to his forehand and back again without moving his feet. When he has mastered the exercise in this part of the court, he should attempt it at a point closer to the front wall, making greater demands on his timing, reflexes, accuracy and endurance.

PRACTICING THE REVERSE CORNER SHOT

Practicing the reverse corner shot (or cross-court corner shot) poses an interesting challenge. To hit the shot on the backhand, the player faces the left side wall in a square stance and bounces the ball against the wall so that it can be hit well in front of his body. The ball, struck hard, hits the right side wall near the front wall, caroms to the front wall and from there flies back to the left side wall. As it bounces from the side wall, it is struck with another sharp backhand so that it returns to the right side wall. If the stroke is made properly, the rectangular pattern of the ball's flight is repeated.

At first the shot should be hit higher on the right side wall than would be tactically sound in a game so that it will return to a point where it can be stroked again from the same position. This exercise, in addition to developing accuracy, serves to give the player a feeling for the diagonal width of the court—a factor in determining the speed and direction necessary for reverse corner shots and cross-court drop shots.

While the reverse corner shot is more often played from the backhand side than from the forehand—the player has a better view of the court from the backhand side—the same exercise can be done with the forehand. In this case, the player faces the right side wall and adopts an open stance.

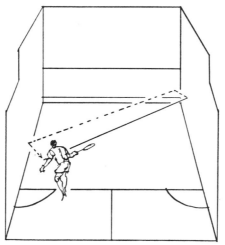

11
Glossary

Ace—A shot which one's opponent cannot touch with his racket

Alley shot—See diagram, p. 95

Backing on the ball—Backing up to take a ball that has hit a side wall, then the back wall, and breaks toward the middle of the court

Boast—See diagram, p. 95

Boast for nick—See diagram, p. 95

Corner shot—See diagram, p. 95

Covering a shot—Placing oneself in a position to block physically various returns by one's opponent

Cross-court shot—See diagram, p. 95

Die—To fail to bounce

Doubles—Squash played by four people (two on a side) in a larger court than singles (45' x 25' as opposed to 32' x 18' 6"). A livelier ball, distinguished by a red dot, is used

Down-the-line shot—Same as alley shot

Drive—A ball hit hard after it bounces

Drop shot—A ball hit softly to the front wall

Fault—A bad serve

Gallery—Spectators' area

Get—Scrambling return of a difficult shot

Half-volley—Ball hit immediately after bouncing

Length—Descriptive of a ball that bounces twice or dies before reaching the back wall

Let—A point that must be replayed

Let point—Point awarded to a player for deliberate interference on the part of his opponent

Lob—A ball hit high on the front wall

Monkey doubles—Doubles played in a singles court with a singles ball but using rackets whose handles have been cut down

Nick—A ball that hits the juncture of the floor and a side wall, or the floor and the back wall, simultaneously, rolling out and therefore impossible to retrieve

No set—Call made optionally by the receiver at 13-all or 14-all (in both of which cases the game is 15)

Philadelphia shot or Philadelphia Boast—A trick shot, a boast in reverse. See diagram, p. 86

Putaway—A shot that cannot be retrieved

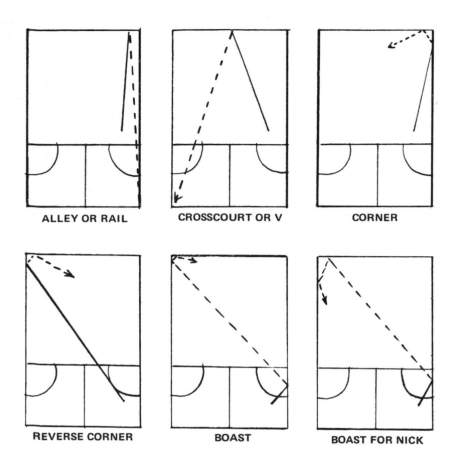

ALLEY OR RAIL   CROSSCOURT OR V   CORNER

REVERSE CORNER   BOAST   BOAST FOR NICK

Quarter circle—Area in which the server places one foot while serving

Rail shot—Same as alley shot

Rally—A series of shots

Reverse corner shot—See diagram above.

Service box—Same as quarter circle

T—That part of the court just in front of the floor service line and the center service line; the most advantageous part of the court from which to hit returns

Telltale—17-inch-high rectangle of sheet metal at the bottom of the front wall that gives off a ringing sound when struck by the ball. The ball must clear it in order to be good

Tin—The telltale

Touch—Player's finesse in hitting corner and drop shots

Turning on the ball—Turning around to take a ball coming off the back wall

Volley—Ball hit before it reaches the floor

Winner—Same as putaway